woman   women   man   men

boy   boys   girl   girls

baby   babies   people

1

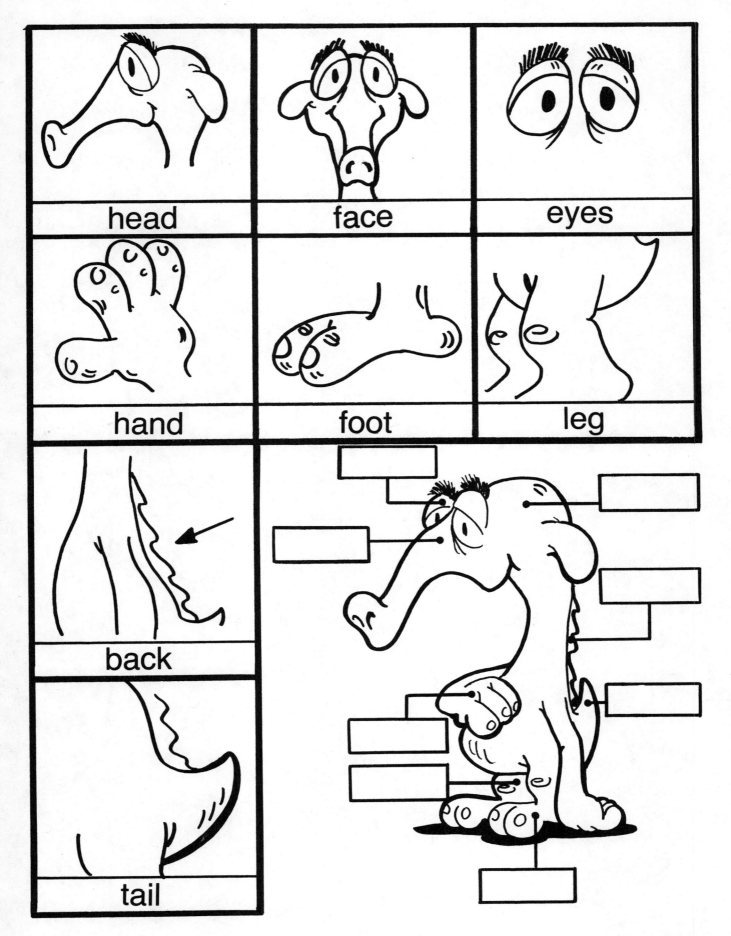

head

face

eyes

hand

foot

leg

back

tail

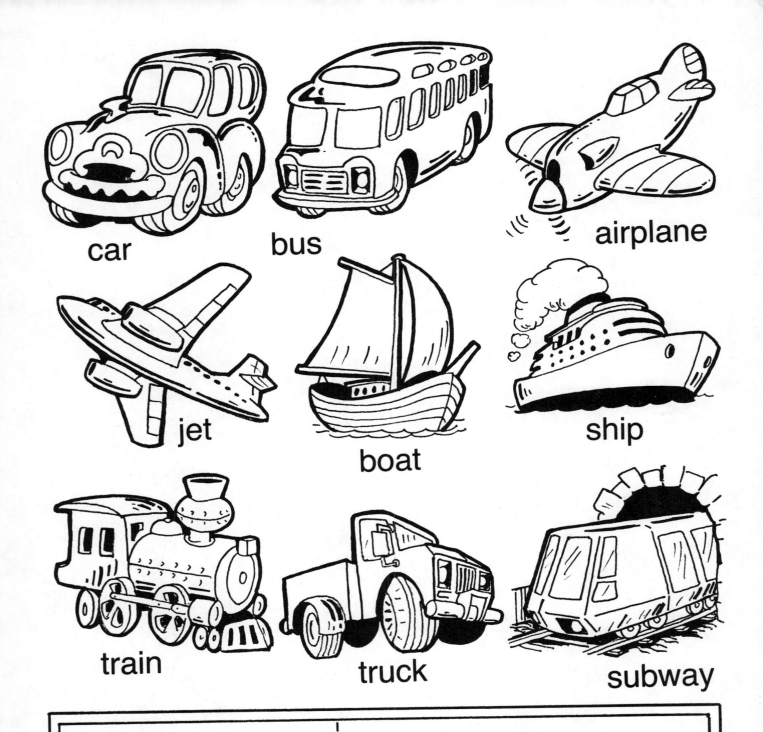

car

bus

airplane

jet

boat

ship

train

truck

subway

Put picture here.

This ticket good for one

_____

ride.

4

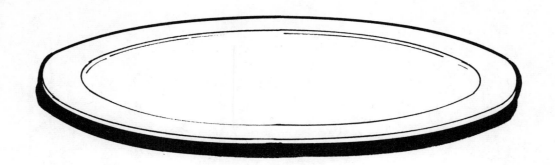

I have _____ on my plate.

apples

bread

cake

cheese

corn

eggs

fish

meat

peas

shirt

mittens

coat

jacket

cap

dress

socks

skirt

shoes

pants

I have on my _____.

5

window

door

steps

table

chair

bed

lamp

clock

picture

books

phone

rug

bike

bat

ball

doll

car

truck

blocks

bear

bank

game

drum

paper

7

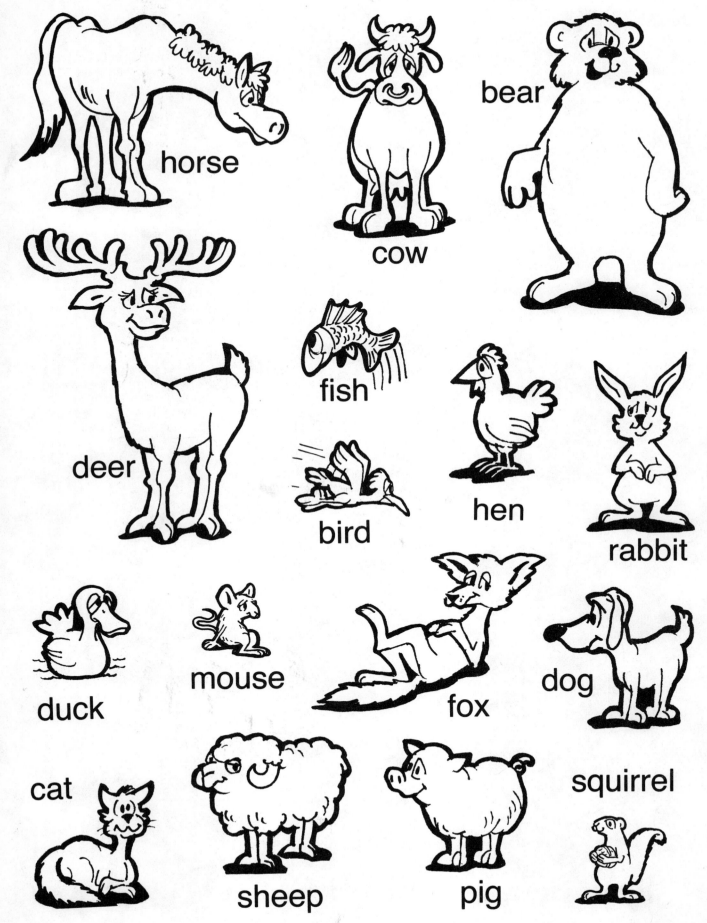

horse

cow

bear

deer

fish

bird

hen

rabbit

duck

mouse

fox

dog

squirrel

cat

sheep

pig

sun

moon

star

cloud

rock

flower

nest

tree

hill

island

lake

walk

run

jump

stand

sit

swim

kick

ride

fly

10

pick up

carry

put down

cook

eat

drink

wash

brush

sleep

11

read

write

draw

cut

make

listen

play

work

help

12

talk

sing

shout

hear

watch

whisper

smile

laugh

cry

think

look

love

13

go

stop

call

come

push

pull

I can . . .

look	eat	jump	sit
talk	wash	fly	watch
laugh	sleep	swim	smile

tall
short
big
little
fat
thin
long

16

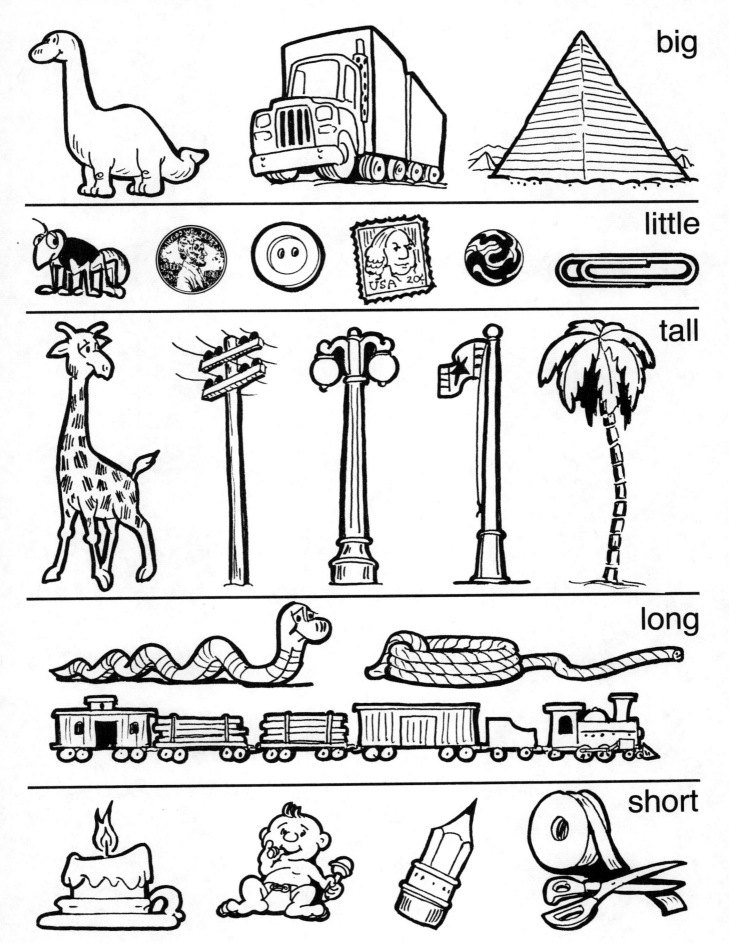

big

little

tall

long

short

17

new

old

fast

slow

clean

dirty

light

heavy

young

old

happy

sad

cold

hot

soft

hard

19

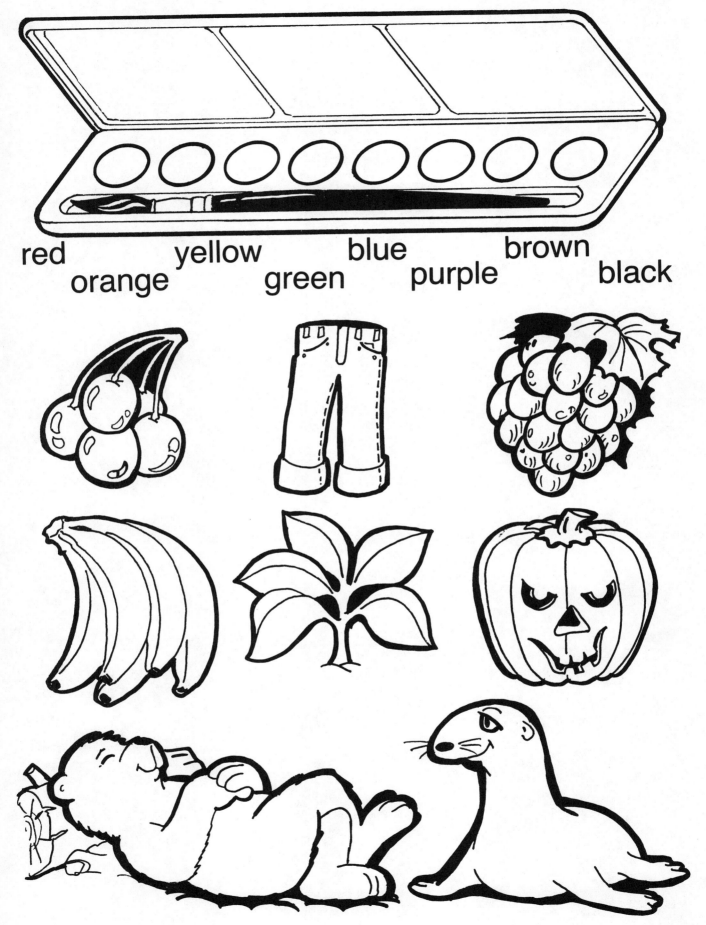

red   yellow   blue   brown

orange   green   purple   black

on

over

under

behind

beside

around

through

cat

fan

pen

hat

pan

hen

mat

can

men

bat

man

ten

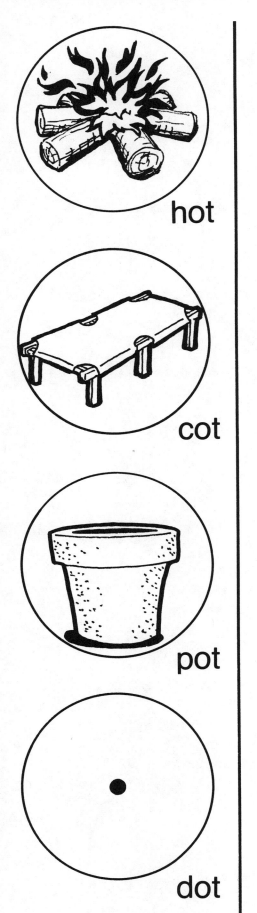

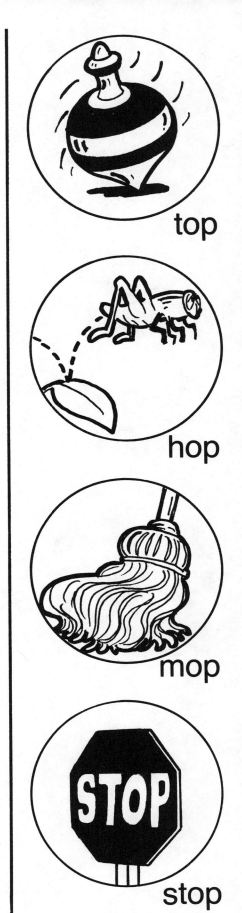

hot

net

top

cot

pet

hop

pot

wet

mop

dot

jet

stop

bug

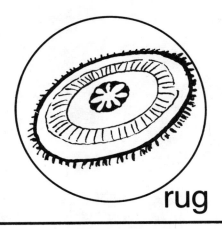
rug

jug

frog

dog

log

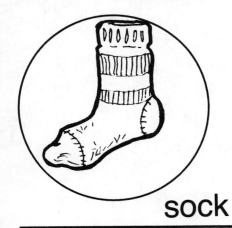
sock

lock

rock

ring

wing

king

pig   wig   fish   dish

box   fox   map   cap

nut   hut   mad   sad

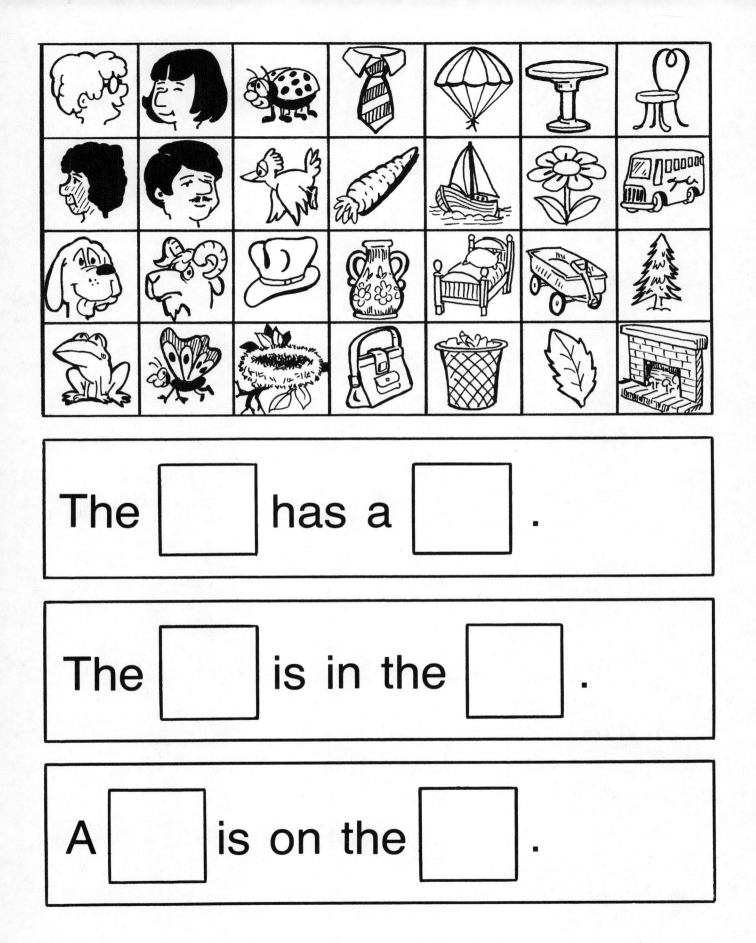

The ☐ has a ☐ .

The ☐ is in the ☐ .

A ☐ is on the ☐ .

27

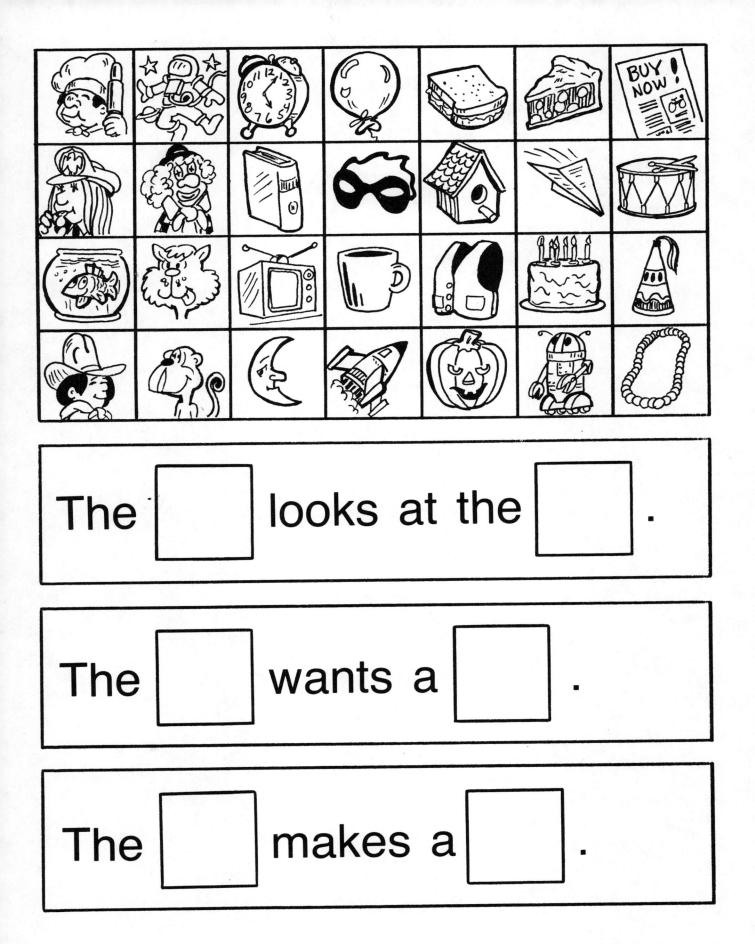

The ☐ looks at the ☐ .

The ☐ wants a ☐ .

The ☐ makes a ☐ .

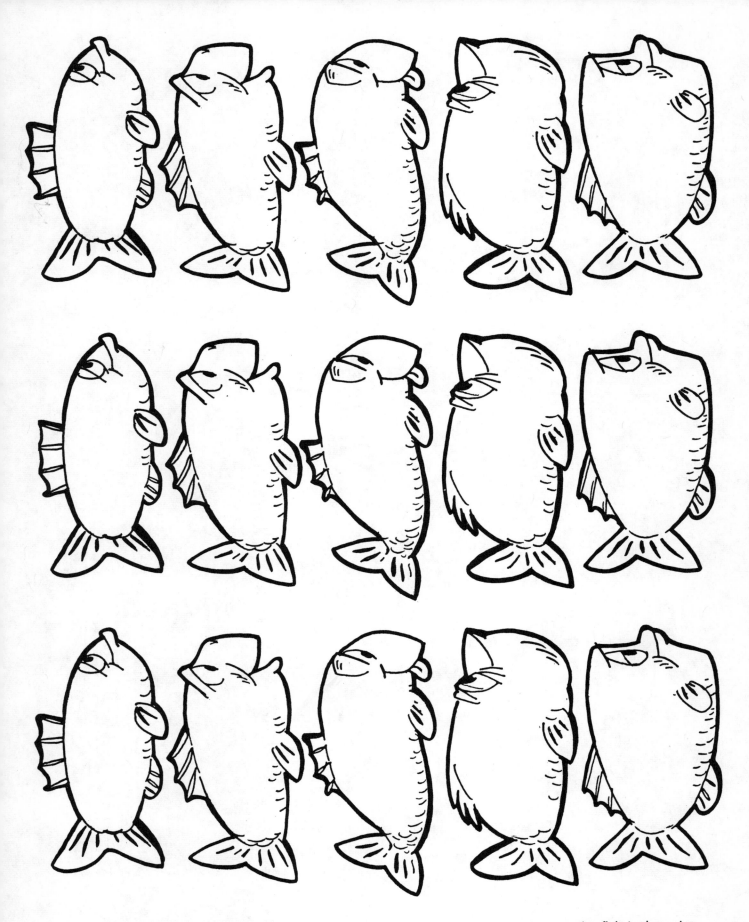

Duplicate and cut out the fish. You or the child can print a word on each fish to paste on the fish tank poster.

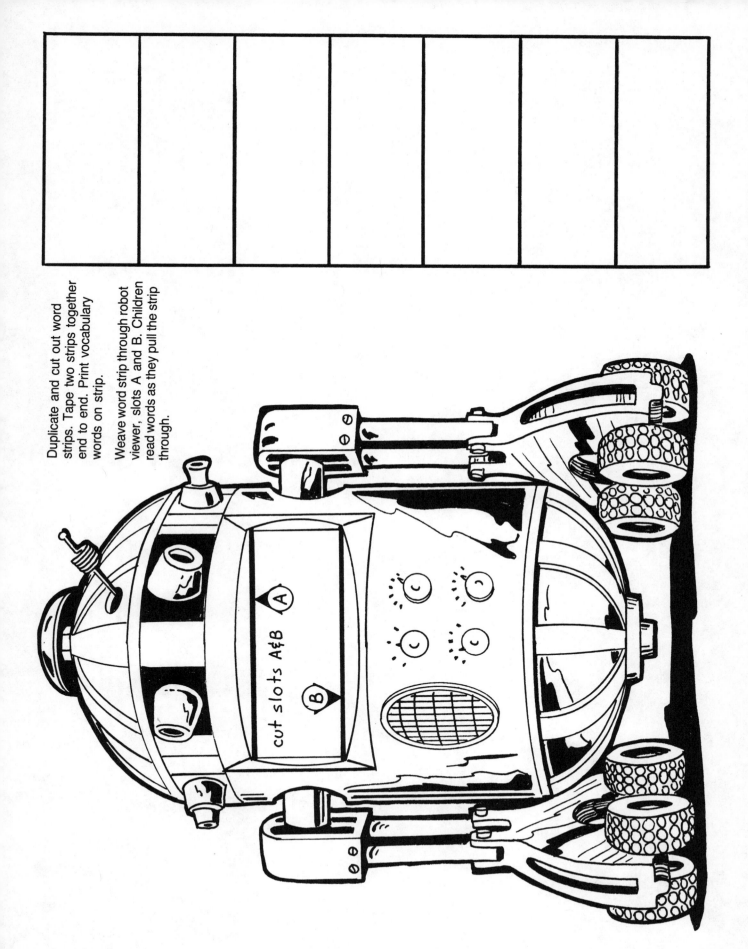

Duplicate and cut out word strips. Tape two strips together end to end. Print vocabulary words on strip.

Weave word strip through robot viewer, slots A and B. Children read words as they pull the strip through.

cut slots A & B

Ⓐ

Ⓑ